DKfindout!
Dinosaurs

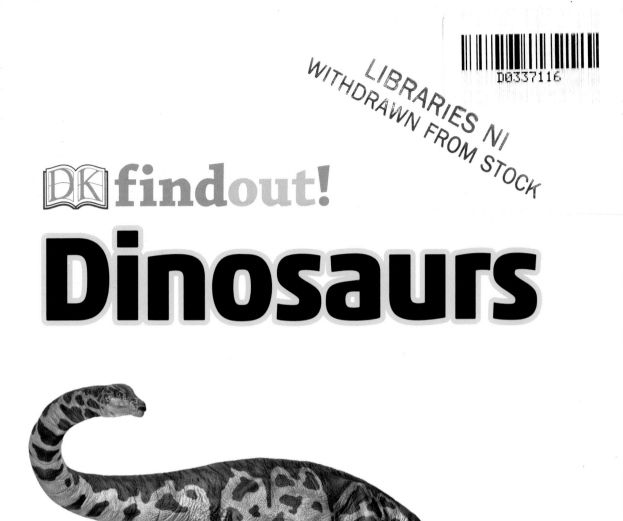

Author: Andrea Mills
Consultant: Dr Darren Naish

DK | Penguin Random House

Editor Olivia Stanford
Project art editor Joanne Clark
Senior editor Gill Pitts
Managing editor Laura Gilbert
Managing art editor Diane Peyton Jones
Picture research Surya Sarangi
Pre-production producer Nadine King
Producer Srijana Gurung
Art director Martin Wilson
Publisher Sarah Larter
Publishing director Sophie Mitchell

Educational consultant Jacqueline Harris

First published in Great Britain in 2016 by
Dorling Kindersley Limited
80 Strand, London, WC2R 0RL

A CIP catalogue record for this book
is available from the British Library.
ISBN: 978-0-2412-5026-6

Printed and bound in China

A WORLD OF IDEAS:
SEE ALL THERE IS TO KNOW

www.dk.com

Contents

Stegosaurus

The scale boxes throughout
the book show you how big a
dinosaur was compared to a
person who is 1.8 m (6 ft) tall.

» Scale

Pterodaustro

Sinosauropteryx

Triceratops

Sauropelta

Diplodocus

Teeth

Meat-eating dinosaurs, such as T. rex, had powerful jaws packed with huge teeth, ready to tear into flesh and bone.

Diplodocus

Neck

Feeding on the tallest treetops was only possible for dinosaurs with very long, flexible necks, like the leaf-loving Diplodocus.

What is a dinosaur?

Millions of years ago, long before humans lived on Earth, a group of remarkable reptiles ruled the planet. Called dinosaurs, which means "terrible lizards", they all lived on land and had clawed hands and feet. However, some dinosaurs had long, pointed teeth, while others had thick, armoured skin, and some had feathers, just like birds today.

Iguanodon

Front limbs

Some dinosaurs had four sturdy legs for walking, while others had two arms and two legs. Iguanodon could walk on either two or four feet.

Plates

Stegosaurus had large plates running along its back. They may have been brightly coloured and used for showing off to other dinosaurs.

Stegosaurus

Velociraptor

Body

Some dinosaurs, such as Velociraptor, were covered in feathers. Birds are descended from dinosaurs.

Ankylosaurus

Tail

Though dinosaur tails helped with balance, one swipe from the muscular, club-like tail of Ankylosaurus could prove deadly to enemies.

Brachiosaurus

Hind legs

Dinosaur legs were positioned directly underneath the body. This meant they could support the huge weight of giant dinosaurs like Brachiosaurus.

Eggs

Female dinosaurs laid clusters of hard-shelled eggs. Some dinosaurs built nests and looked after their young.

Sizing them up

Dinosaurs have a reputation for being the biggest and fiercest creatures ever to inhabit this planet. While it is true that many were larger than a house, some were as small as a chicken. Scientific research has revealed the incredible range of sizes of these reptiles, and how each of the dinosaurs measured up.

Triceratops
Even though Triceratops was an average-sized dinosaur, it was still as long as two cars.

Sinosauropteryx
This little carnivore was a fast hunter, running on two feet. Sinosauropteryx grew to just 1 m (3 ft) long, which is about twice the size of a cat.

How do we know?

Dinosaurs died out 66 million years ago, so how do we know so much about them? Fortunately, scientists have found lots of dinosaur fossils, mainly of their bones. By examining their preserved bones and the tracks they left behind, experts can tell how large a dinosaur was, what it ate, how it lived, and even how it may have died.

95 million-year-old dinosaur bones

Looking at bones
Dinosaur experts take their finds back to the laboratory to find out more about them. The bones shown here are from a sauropod, a group of long-necked dinosaurs that were some of the biggest to ever walk the Earth.

Argentinosaurus

This super-sized dinosaur is one of the largest ever found. Argentinosaurus was as long as three buses and would have towered over a two-storey building.

Fossilized dinosaur footprints

Following in their footsteps

Scientists can learn a lot from dinosaur footprints. They reveal the dinosaur's size, whether it walked on two or four legs, the speed at which it was moving, and whether it was alone or travelling in a herd.

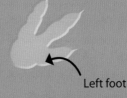

Left foot

Right foot

Distance between the heel of each foot gives the length of the dinosaur's stride.

Dinosaur world

The Mesozoic Era is the name for the time when dinosaurs dominated the Earth. Lasting for over 180 million years, this enormous era is divided into three time periods called the Triassic, Jurassic, and Cretaceous. As the climate changed and new types of plants grew, different animals appeared. To describe when these periods were we shorten "million years ago" to MYA.

Jurassic period

The Jurassic period (201–145 MYA) saw changing seasons. A combination of high temperatures and rainfall caused flourishing forests. The lush vegetation included tall trees and widespread plants, providing a reliable food supply for huge plant-eating dinosaurs.

Pleuromeia, a type of tree-like plant, grew to 2 m (6 ft).

Plateosaurus

Stegosaurus

Allosaurus

Coelophysis

Triassic period

The Triassic period (252–201 MYA) was the hottest time in dinosaur history. The dry, desert landscape was bare, except for plants growing by riverbanks and coastlines. Small dinosaurs and tiny mammals began to appear on the Earth for the first time.

Eoraptor

Insects like dragonflies and beetles flew through the air.

Creepy-crawlies including spiders, scorpions, and millipedes had appeared before the Triassic period.

Pterodactylus was a flying reptile that lived in the Jurassic period.

Conifers, like this monkey puzzle tree, thrived.

Brachiosaurus

Cretaceous period

The final age of dinosaurs was the Cretaceous period (145–66 MYA), bringing a drop in temperature. The warm and wet weather produced rainforests and the first flowers bloomed. Plant-eating dinosaurs developed body armour to protect themselves against the fierce meat-eating dinosaurs.

Grass appears at the end of the Cretaceous period.

Tyrannosaurus rex

Triceratops

Many types of insect, including bees, arrive.

Answer the questions to find out which group an individual dinosaur belongs to.

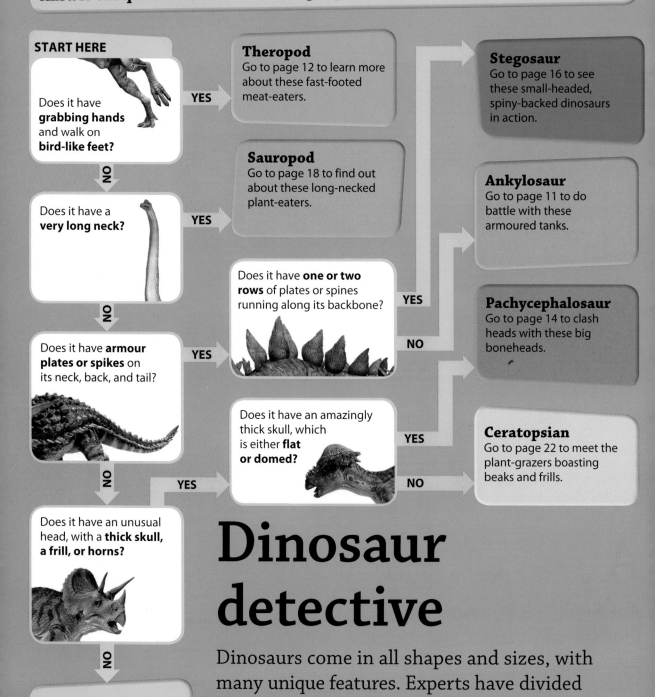

START HERE

Does it have **grabbing hands** and walk on **bird-like feet?**

YES →

Theropod
Go to page 12 to learn more about these fast-footed meat-eaters.

NO

Does it have a **very long neck?**

YES →

Sauropod
Go to page 18 to find out about these long-necked plant-eaters.

NO

Does it have **armour plates or spikes** on its neck, back, and tail?

YES →

Does it have **one or two rows** of plates or spines running along its backbone?

YES → **Stegosaur**
Go to page 16 to see these small-headed, spiny-backed dinosaurs in action.

NO →

Does it have an amazingly thick skull, which is either **flat or domed?**

YES → **Pachycephalosaur**
Go to page 14 to clash heads with these big boneheads.

NO → **Ankylosaur**
Go to page 11 to do battle with these armoured tanks.

NO

YES →

Does it have an unusual head, with a **thick skull, a frill, or horns?**

YES → **Ceratopsian**
Go to page 22 to meet the plant-grazers boasting beaks and frills.

NO

Ornithopod
Go to page 20 to catch up with these agile plant-eaters.

Dinosaur detective

Dinosaurs come in all shapes and sizes, with many unique features. Experts have divided them into seven types, which share certain characteristics. When you know the difference, you can become a dinosaur detective and work out which one belongs to which group.

FACT FILE

» **When:** Early Cretaceous

» **Length:** 7 m (23 ft)

» **Fun fact:** Sauropelta had a horny beak instead of front teeth.

Sauropelta

A scary sight, Sauropelta was huge, heavy, and came complete with horn-covered plates. This ankylosaur had extra defensive weapons, including sharp spikes and spines on its shoulders.

WOW!

The best way to **injure Sauropelta** was to **flip it over** and expose its unplated belly.

Bony studs provided a protective shield.

Sharp blades stood out on either side of the tail.

Spikes were largest and sharpest around the neck.

» Scale

Ankylosaurs

Ankylosaurs had the best protection of any dinosaur. Although they were slow-moving plant-eaters, their self-defence was full body armour. Bony plates that were fused, or joined, to the skin meant that the ankylosaurs, which means "fused lizard", were the last meal choice for any hungry hunters.

Armoured animals

Some of today's animals, such as turtles, crocodiles, and armadillos, also have special types of body armour. Pangolins are covered in hard, overlapping scales and can roll into a ball to protect their belly.

Pangolin

Theropods

This group of powerful predators boasted some of the deadliest dinosaurs ever to walk the Earth. Theropod means "beast-footed" and these killing machines moved on two legs. They were equipped with fierce jaws and sharp claws to help bring down their prey.

! WOW!

Tyrannosaurus rex could swallow up to **225 kg (500 lb) of meat** in one go.

Tail stretched 5 m (16 ft), helping to balance the heavy head.

Tyrannosaurus rex

This frightening reptile killed and scavenged its way to the top of the Cretaceous food chain. It was armed with more than 60 bone-crushing teeth – the strongest of any meat-eating dinosaur.

Biggest teeth were about 20 cm (8 in) long.

Only two sharp-clawed fingers at the end of each small, muscular arm.

» Scale

FACT FILE

» **When:** Late Cretaceous

» **Length:** 12 m (40 ft)

» **Fun fact:** Tyrannosaurus rex had a big brain by dinosaur standards, which made it a good hunter.

Therizinosaurus

This beaky giant was covered in feathers and equipped with long claws. It was one of very few theropods to have a herbivorous (plant-based) diet.

FACT FILE

» **When:** Late Cretaceous

» **Length:** 10 m (33 ft)

» **Fun fact:** Reaching almost 1 m (3 ft), its vicious claws kept predators away.

» Scale

Allosaurus

On the attack, Allosaurus grabbed and slashed its victims before tearing into the flesh. This dinosaur may have hunted in packs to bring down larger prey.

» Scale

FACT FILE

» **When:** Late Jurassic

» **Length:** 8 m (26 ft)

» **Fun fact:** Fossil remains show that Allosaurus occasionally ate one another.

Spinosaurus

This dinosaur is the largest land carnivore (meat-eater) ever recorded. It was the only dinosaur specialized for swimming, allowing it to hunt for fish in rivers.

FACT FILE

» **When:** Late Cretaceous

» **Length:** 16 m (52 ft)

» **Fun fact:** Spinosaurus was four times the weight of an elephant.

» Scale

Bonehead
Surrounded by bony spikes, the thick dome covered the top of the skull and protected the brain.

Forward-facing eyes provided excellent vision.

Wide hips suggest that they had big guts.

Spikes
Bony spikes along the snout may have been used to injure rivals or predators.

Long, powerful back legs allowed this dinosaur to run fast when it needed to.

Pachycephalosaurs

Pachycephalosaur means "thick-headed lizard" and these dinosaurs were instantly recognizable by the great domes of bone growing from their skulls. They were herbivores (plant-eaters) and travelled on two legs, searching forests for fruits and leaves.

Skin

The skin of Pachycephalosaurus probably had a bumpy surface but little evidence survives so we can't know for sure.

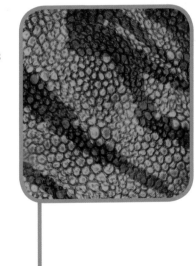

Butting battles

Some people think male pachycephalosaurs used their heads to fight for females. It is believed that they banged their bony heads together in head-butting contests. Today, wild sheep and goats behave in the same way, clashing horns to find out who is stronger.

Two male sheep butting heads

Toes

The clawed, four-toed feet were spread out to help take the dinosaur's weight as it walked on two legs.

The tail had rod-like bones with muscles sitting between them. This feature is usually seen in fish.

FACT FILE

» **When:** Late Cretaceous

» **Length:** 5 m (16 ft)

» **Fun fact:** The skull of Pachycephalosaurus was so thick that its fossilized remains have been found long after the rest of its bones have broken down.

Pachycephalosaurus

Meet the largest domed dinosaur of all. Pachycephalosaurus had an incredibly thick, 25 cm (10 in) high bone dome. It might have used it for defence against predators like Tyrannosaurus rex.

! WOW!

The skull of a Pachycephalosaurus was at least **20 times thicker** than other dinosaur skulls.

Stegosaurus

This dinosaur showed off the distinctive bony plates along its spine to impress rivals. Stegosaurus ate huge amounts of plants to sustain its massive size.

The bony plates may also have worked like solar panels, absorbing the Sun's warmth.

» Scale

The tail of this dinosaur took up almost half of its entire body length.

Sharp tail spikes were up to 90 cm (35 in) long and were used for self-defence.

Stegosaurs

These armoured dinosaurs moved slowly and ate only plants, but they were a terrifying prospect for predators. Stegosaur means "roof lizard", and many of them displayed two rows of huge bony plates standing up along their backbone. They used their spiky tails to swipe at attackers.

Kentrosaurus

Bulky Kentrosaurus was one of the spikiest of the stegosaurs, making an attack challenging for even the most confident predator.

» Scale

Huayangosaurus

Small by stegosaur standards, Huayangosaurus had short front legs and longer back legs. This made it easier to bend down to graze on plants.

» Scale

Scutellosaurus

Smaller than you, this tiny dinosaur resembled a modern-day lizard. Scutellosaurus wasn't a stegosaur itself, but it was closely related to them.

» Scale

Sauropods

The skyscraping sauropods were the largest land animals to have ever lived on our planet. These plant-eating dinosaurs had healthy appetites to match their huge size. Using their incredibly long necks to reach the leafiest treetops, they fed continually to fuel their enormous bodies.

FACT FILE

» **When:** Late Jurassic

» **Length:** 27 m (88 ft)

» **Fun fact:** The whip-like tail of Diplodocus could be used to keep away attackers.

Long tail might have propped up Diplodocus when rearing up.

» Scale

Diplodocus

Walking tall in the Jurassic world, Diplodocus could dine on the highest trees. Like all sauropods, it stripped leaves from branches and swallowed them whole.

Brachiosaurus

Brachiosaurus had longer front legs than any other sauropod. It could stretch to 15 m (49 ft) to feed. Its enormous stomach helped it get energy from its leafy diet.

» Scale

FACT FILE

» **When:** Late Jurassic

» **Length:** 25 m (82 ft)

» **Fun fact:** Brachiosaurus swallowed about 200 kg (440 lb) of leaves every day.

Apatosaurus

This big sauropod fed on the many conifer trees that grew in the Jurassic period. Apatosaurus had an extra thick, strong neck, with bony lumps that may have been used for fighting.

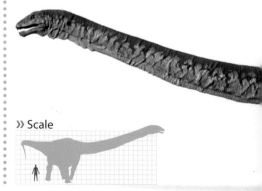

» Scale

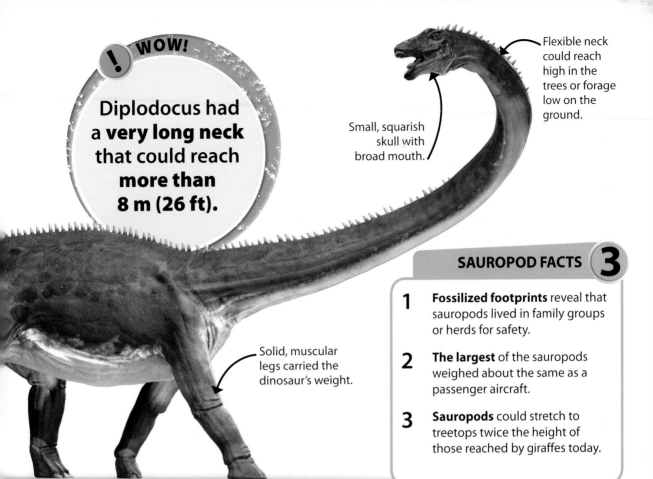

WOW!

Diplodocus had a **very long neck** that could reach **more than 8 m (26 ft).**

Flexible neck could reach high in the trees or forage low on the ground.

Small, squarish skull with broad mouth.

Solid, muscular legs carried the dinosaur's weight.

SAUROPOD FACTS **3**

1 **Fossilized footprints** reveal that sauropods lived in family groups or herds for safety.

2 **The largest** of the sauropods weighed about the same as a passenger aircraft.

3 **Sauropods** could stretch to treetops twice the height of those reached by giraffes today.

FACT FILE

» **When:** Late Jurassic

» **Length:** 21 m (69 ft)

» **Fun fact:** The front feet of Apatosaurus had a big, curved thumb claw but no other claws.

Saltasaurus

Small for a sauropod, Saltasaurus was covered in bony knobs and spines. This may have been protective body armour because its small size made it an easier target.

» Scale

FACT FILE

» **When:** Late Cretaceous

» **Length:** 12 m (40 ft)

» **Fun fact:** Saltasaurus was named after the Salta area in Argentina where the first of these dinosaurs was found.

Ornithopods

Ornithopod means "bird feet" and many of these dinosaurs were small and speedy. Some switched between walking on two or four legs. Although they were bulky, ornithopods were plant-eaters and many had beaks for collecting leaves. Some may have lived in herds for safety.

Iguanodon

This huge ornithopod had a sharp thumb spike on each hand to defend itself against predators. Iguanodon was the first plant-eating dinosaur discovered, with fossils found in England in 1822.

Fossil hand showing thumb spike on the right.

Each bony thumb spike measured 14 cm (6 in) long.

Hypsilophodon

Faced with the decision of fight or flight, this small ornithopod had a choice. It could flee at speed or bite or kick its attacker with the claws on its toes.

FACT FILE

» **When:** Early Cretaceous

» **Length:** 2 m (6 ft)

» **Fun fact:** Scientists once thought that Hypsilophodon lived in the trees.

Ouranosaurus

The sweltering heat of Africa was home for duck-billed Ouranosaurus. A large, spiny sail running along its back might have been boldly patterned and was probably used as a display feature.

» Scale

Heavy tail was raised off the ground for stability.

» Scale

Strong hind limbs gave the option of moving on two or four legs.

Past mistakes

Historic ideas about dinosaurs were sometimes wrong. These Iguanodon models were based on fossils found in 1822. It shows them as big lizards and, as no skull was found, the thumb bone was thought to be a nose horn.

FACT FILE

» **When:** Early Cretaceous

» **Length:** 9 m (30 ft)

» **Fun fact:** Iguanodon means "iguana teeth" because its giant gnashers look like a modern iguana's, but they're 20 times bigger!

Iguanodon models in Crystal Palace Park, England, from the 1800s.

FACT FILE

» **When:** Early Cretaceous

» **Length:** 7 m (23 ft)

» **Fun fact:** A bony bump in front of each eye made Ouranosaurus the only horned ornithopod.

Parasaurolophus

You would hear Parasaurolophus coming from a long way off! It had a hollow crest on its head, which made its calls reverberate, making them louder. This dinosaur roamed in herds, using its horny beak to feed on plants.

FACT FILE

» **When:** Late Cretaceous

» **Length:** 12 m (40 ft)

» **Fun fact:** Scientists once thought that Parasaurolophus lived in water, using its crest as a snorkel!

» Scale

» Scale

Ceratopsians

The spectacular heads of ceratopsians stood out from all the other types of dinosaur. Ceratopsian means "horned face" and their horns and frills provided a protective shield around the head. These four-legged plant-eaters also used their distinctive facial features for display.

Triceratops

Like a giant rhinoceros with three horns, Triceratops was built like a tank. It was well-equipped to deter predators with its overwhelming size, vast frill, and spiky horns.

Tail shorter than that of most other dinosaurs.

Triceratops walked on four legs.

Udanoceratops

An unusual ceratopsian, Udanoceratops had no face horns at all and only a small neck frill. With a sturdy beak, it could feed on the tough leaves of ferns.

» Scale

FACT FILE

» **When:** Late Cretaceous

» **Length:** 4 m (13 ft)

» **Fun fact:** We only know about Udanoceratops from two fossils found in Mongolia.

Einiosaurus

This ceratopsian was a stunning sight with a long, curved horn on its snout. It had bony ridges above its eyes, and two spiky horns sticking out from a neck frill with a wavy edge. Einiosaurus travelled in herds to protect themselves against predators.

» Scale

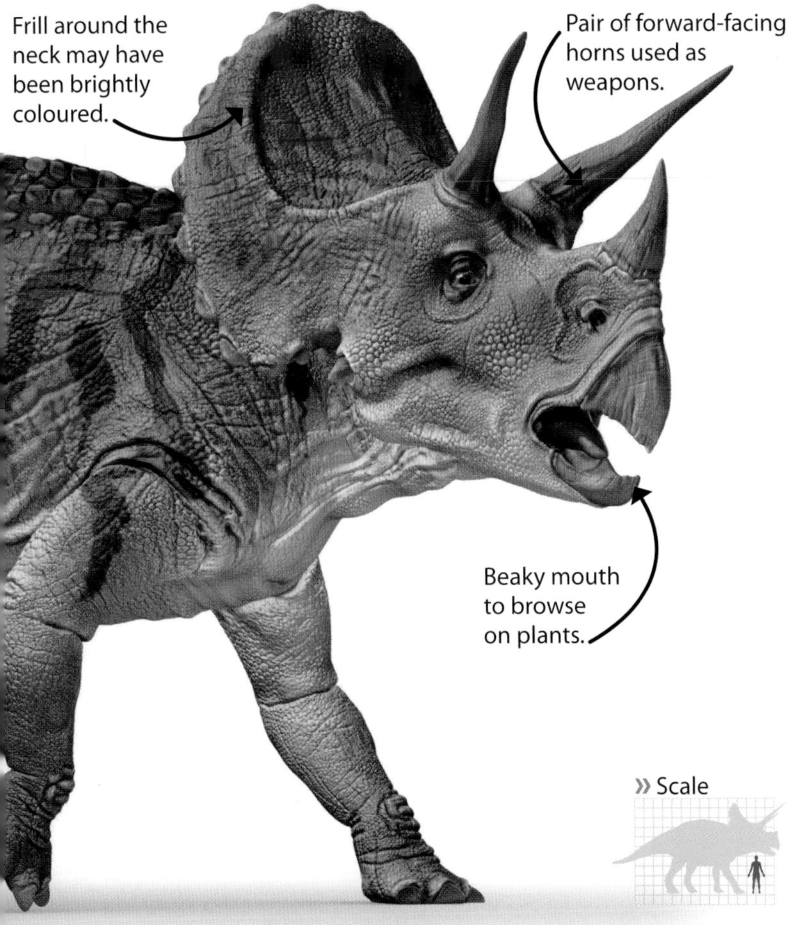

Frill around the neck may have been brightly coloured.

Pair of forward-facing horns used as weapons.

Beaky mouth to browse on plants.

» Scale

! WOW!

Triceratops fought **fierce duels** with rivals by charging and locking horns!

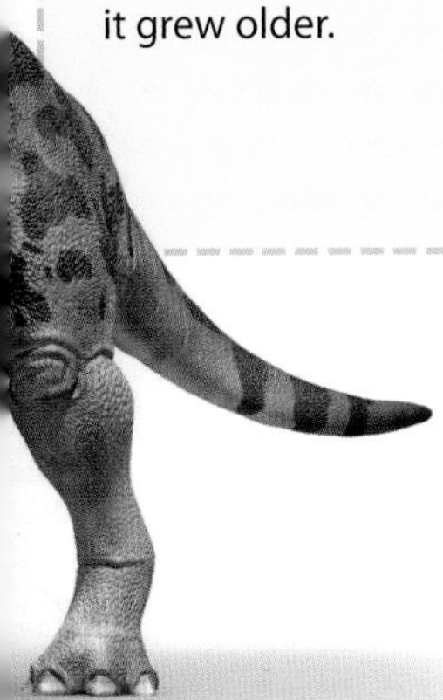

Pentaceratops

With five horns on its face, including a horn on each cheek, Pentaceratops was able to charge at predators and inflict serious damage. A tough beak could tear through plants like leafy ferns easily.

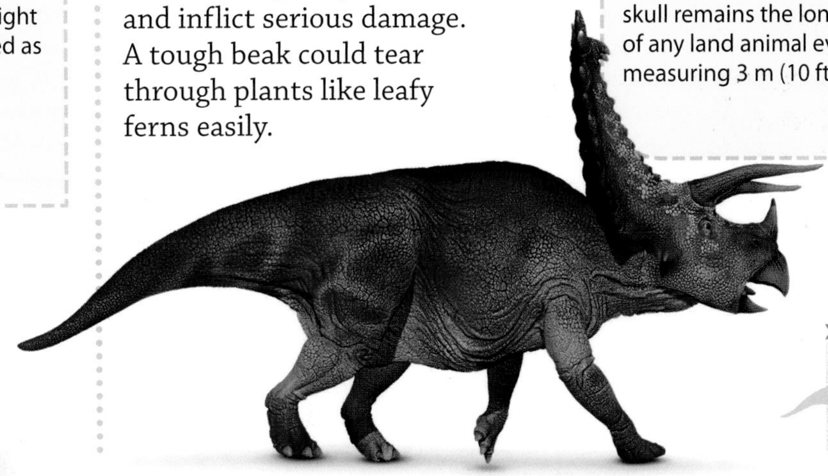

» Scale

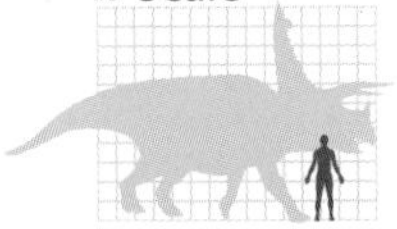

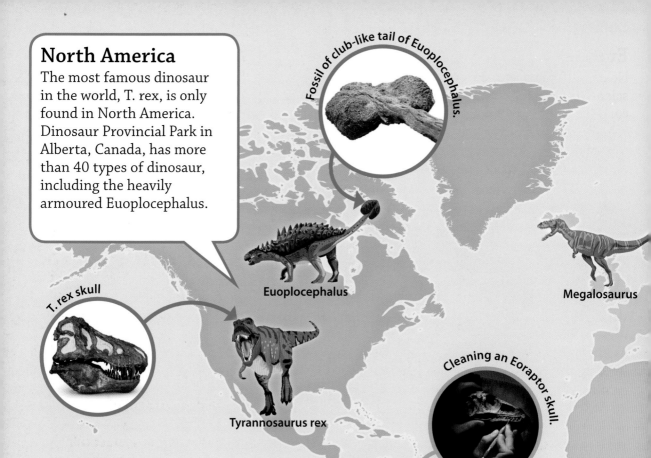

North America

The most famous dinosaur in the world, T. rex, is only found in North America. Dinosaur Provincial Park in Alberta, Canada, has more than 40 types of dinosaur, including the heavily armoured Euoplocephalus.

Fossil of club-like tail of Euoplocephalus.

T. rex skull

Euoplocephalus

Megalosaurus

Tyrannosaurus rex

Cleaning an Eoraptor skull.

Eoraptor

Saltasaurus

Where are they found?

Dinosaur remains have been found on every continent of the world. Some sites are particularly exciting, with more than 10,000 bones being discovered. These include places where rocks have been worn away naturally, exposing the remains, or cut away by human activity, such as in quarries.

South America

South America was home to some of the earliest dinosaurs, including Eoraptor. The continent also boasts some of the largest dinosaurs, such as Saltasaurus.

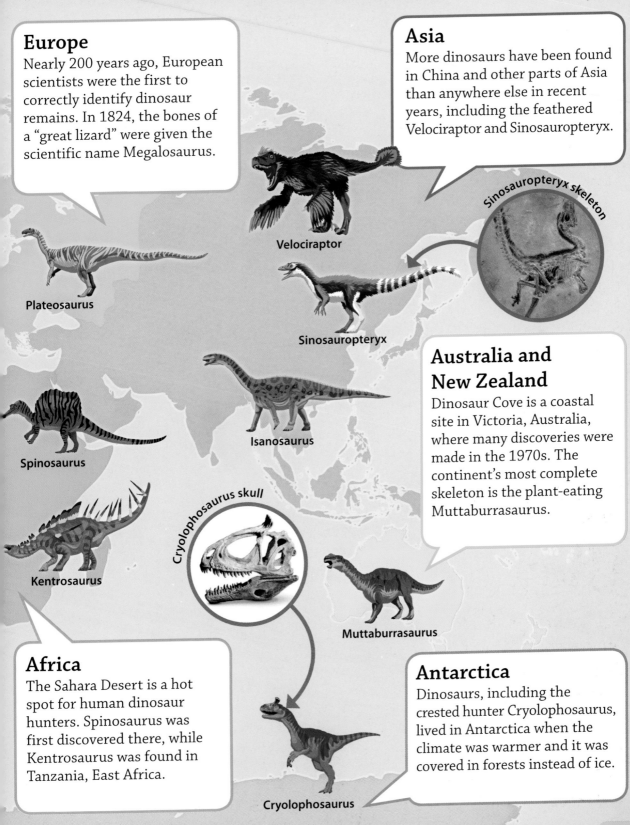

Europe

Nearly 200 years ago, European scientists were the first to correctly identify dinosaur remains. In 1824, the bones of a "great lizard" were given the scientific name Megalosaurus.

Asia

More dinosaurs have been found in China and other parts of Asia than anywhere else in recent years, including the feathered Velociraptor and Sinosauropteryx.

Velociraptor

Sinosauropteryx skeleton

Plateosaurus

Sinosauropteryx

Australia and New Zealand

Dinosaur Cove is a coastal site in Victoria, Australia, where many discoveries were made in the 1970s. The continent's most complete skeleton is the plant-eating Muttaburrasaurus.

Spinosaurus

Isanosaurus

Cryolophosaurus skull

Kentrosaurus

Muttaburrasaurus

Africa

The Sahara Desert is a hot spot for human dinosaur hunters. Spinosaurus was first discovered there, while Kentrosaurus was found in Tanzania, East Africa.

Antarctica

Dinosaurs, including the crested hunter Cryolophosaurus, lived in Antarctica when the climate was warmer and it was covered in forests instead of ice.

Cryolophosaurus

Fossilization

The process of fossilization turns dinosaur remains into stone. Some dead dinosaurs became buried under layers of mud over many millions of years. Chemical changes caused their bones to be replaced with stone. These fossils are rocky replicas of dinosaurs, preserving the past for all time. This gives palaeontologists, who are scientists that study fossils, an incredible opportunity to see what they looked like.

Surrounding mud and ash.

The dead body of an Allosaurus in its muddy resting place.

147 MILLION YEARS AGO

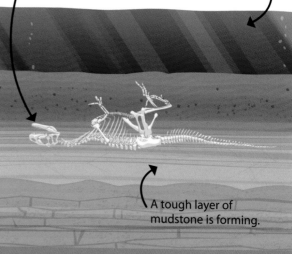

The bones of Allosaurus move about with the settling sediment.

A lake has formed over the bones.

A tough layer of mudstone is forming.

100 MILLION YEARS AGO

Death

This Allosaurus died at the end of the Jurassic period from sickness, old age, or injury. Its body lies in soft mud by a shallow river, while a distant, erupting volcano pours lava and ash onto the land. If scavengers stay away, the fossilization process can begin.

Burial

The river carries sediments like mud, sand, and ash, which cover the dinosaur's body. The flesh and organs rot away, leaving only bones behind. Over millions of years, more layers of sediment are added, and heat and pressure build up, causing the layers to harden into solid rock called mudstone.

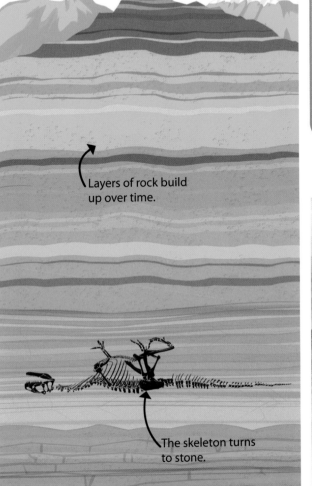

Mountains may form on top of the older layers of rock.

Layers of rock build up over time.

The skeleton turns to stone.

2 MILLION YEARS AGO

Mineralization

Minerals in the ground enter the bones and over time are turned into rock. The Allosaurus is turned to stone, like the surrounding layers of sediment. The top layers of rock begin to erode (wear down) as rain, wind, and frost break them up and wash them away.

Trace fossils

Body fossils, like skeletons, are a direct look at dinosaurs themselves, but other remains also provide information. Trace fossils are preserved signs of life, such as footprints and dung. These build a picture of how dinosaurs walked, lived, and fed.

Coprolites
Coprolites are fossilized dung. Some still contain the remains of the dinosaur's last meal!

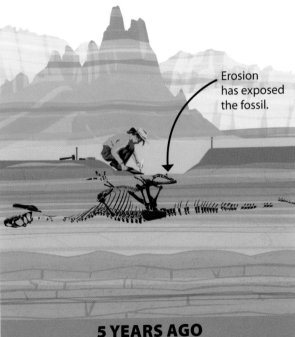

Erosion has exposed the fossil.

5 YEARS AGO

Discovery

A palaeontologist spots a bone sticking out of the ground and discovers the dinosaur. An Allosaurus from the Jurassic period! Erosion has continued to wear down and carry away the rock around the Allosaurus until part of it is visible. The rest of the skeleton can then be carefully dug up.

Meet the expert

We put some questions to Dr Kenneth Lacovara, a palaeontologist at Rowan University in New Jersey, USA. He is famous for discovering the super-massive sauropod Dreadnoughtus in Argentina in 2005.

Q: We know it is something to do with dinosaurs, but what is your actual job?

A: I travel to faraway places to dig up dinosaur fossils. My team spends months chipping away at rocks to reveal the fossilized bones. Before moving the fossils, we protect them with a "jacket" made of plaster and a material called hessian.

Q: What made you decide to become a palaeontologist?

A: As a child, I became fascinated with the ancient past. I studied geology in college to learn more about Earth's history. When I realized that I could make a living digging up and studying dinosaurs, I was hooked.

Dreadnoughtus
This dinosaur was named Dreadnoughtus, which means "fears nothing", because it was too large for any predator to prey on it. Dreadnoughtus weighed 59 tonnes (65 tons) when it died and was still growing fast!

Dr Lacovara lies next to the shin bone of Dreadnoughtus.

Q: How do you know where to look for dinosaur fossils?

A: First, find rocks of the right age. Dinosaurs lived from 235 to 66 million years ago, during the Mesozoic Era. Fossils are only found in rocks formed by sediments, such as mud. Don't bother looking for fossils in volcanic rocks or in rocks that have been heated and squeezed by the Earth's crust. They won't be there! Finally, look in deserts, where erosion is constantly uncovering new bones. If you find those three things, walk, keep your eyes on the ground, and be patient. You will almost always find fossils.

Q: What sort of tools do you use?

A: In the field, we use simple tools, such as pickaxes, shovels, hammers, and chisels. In the laboratory, our tools are high-tech. Robotics, 3-D scanners, 3-D printers, and medical equipment all help us to understand dinosaurs and the way they lived.

Dr Lacovara stands next to the curving neck bones.

Digging up Dreadnoughtus
It took the team five years to dig up the remains of the super-massive Dreadnoughtus. More than 70 per cent of its bones were found.

Q: How do you know what dinosaurs looked like in real life?

A: We know their shape from how their bones fit together. Scars on the bones show us where muscles were. Sometimes armour plates, spines, and spikes are preserved and even scales and feathers. To understand parts that do not fossilize, like lungs and eyes, we look at birds, which are descended from dinosaurs, and also crocodiles.

Q: Do you have a favourite dinosaur?

A: Dreadnoughtus! After spending 10 years digging up and studying it, it has become a member of my family. For sheer coolness, though, nothing beats Spinosaurus.

Q: What do you love most about palaeontology?

A: With only a shovel, palaeontology allows you to "time-travel" to ancient landscapes that existed before humans, when the world was ruled by Nature alone.

The total length of Dreadnoughtus was 26 m (85 ft).

Its neck was 11.3 m (37 ft) long.

Skeletons

Dinosaur skeletons could support enormous bodies, providing a strong and stable frame. These bony structures also protected the vital organs like the heart and lungs. Fossilized skeletons show us how dinosaurs might have looked and moved.

Window in the skull, called a fenestra, made the skeleton lighter.

Albertosaurus skeleton

This big, scary predator was a fast mover, especially when hunting prey. The skeleton shows a body built for speed, with two strong back legs. Albertosaurus could grow to 9 m (30 ft) long.

The eye sockets faced slightly forward, which helped when judging the distance to a prey animal!

The large jaws would have had powerful muscles attached to them for a strong bite.

The gastralia were extra ribs that may have helped with breathing.

Claws

Dinosaur claws could be used to attack prey or defend against predators. Hungry meat-eaters stabbed their victims with sharp claws, while threatened plant-eaters wounded attackers with claws just as deadly.

Killer claw
The meat-eating Velociraptor had an enormous curved claw on each foot, used to rip open prey.

Theropods like Albertosaurus are described as "lizard-hipped". Their hips are a different shape to other dinosaurs that are "bird-hipped".

The backbones, or vertebrae, ran all the way down the tail. Humans have a tail bone called the coccyx.

The knees were always bent.

Standing tall

Dinosaur limbs were arranged differently to those of most living reptiles. The position of an animal's legs, their stance, affects how much weight they can carry.

Dinosaur stance
Dinosaurs stood upright with their legs placed directly under their bodies for support, like mammals.

Crocodile stance
Crocodiles have limbs bent at the joint, which do not support weight as well.

Lizard stance
Small reptiles like lizards have limbs that stick out sideways. Their bellies often touch the ground.

The big toe, or hallux, was at the side of the foot.

The feet were suited to running, and clawed toes were spread out for balance.

Defensive claw
The plant-eating Therizinosaurus used its huge, slashing claws to protect against any aggressive predators.

WOW!

A titanosaur thigh bone is the **largest dinosaur bone ever found** at 2.4 m (8 ft) long.

Diet and teeth

Looking inside a dinosaur's mouth reveals plenty about their diet. The shape of the jaw and the types of teeth reflect what was on the prehistoric menu. While meat-eaters had pointed teeth, plant-eaters had beaks or peg-like teeth.

Front teeth stripped leaves.

Rows of razor sharp teeth.

Suchomimus

Herbivores

Many plant-eating herbivores had a horny beak to collect leaves from plants. Others, like the giant Giraffatitan, had rows of spoon-shaped, blunt teeth designed to nip the leaves from tall trees. They swallowed their dinner without chewing!

Carnivores

Meat-eaters had pointed teeth. These were used to slice up chunks of meat or crunch through bone. Suchomimus had a long jaw filled with more than 100 curving teeth that were perfect for keeping hold of slippery fish.

Omnivore

A few dinosaurs were omnivores, eating both animals and plants. They needed more than one kind of tooth in their mouths to deal with their varied diet. Heterodontosaurus, meaning "different-toothed lizard", had a beak and teeth for chopping up plants, and sharp tusks that may have been used to tear meat.

Heterodontosaurus

Beak helps to tear food.

Giant teeth

This terrifying 20 cm (8 in) tooth belonged to T. rex. This monster carnivore had huge jaws, which contained up to 60 pointed teeth. They were strong enough to bite clean through bone and to tackle the heavy armour of ankylosaurs like Ankylosaurus. A bite from a T. rex was 50 times more powerful than a human's!

Long neck to reach tall trees.

Pointed tip and serrated edge.

LIFE SIZE!

! WOW!

Dinosaurs continually **grew and replaced** their teeth throughout their lives.

Carnivore teeth were often chipped and damaged by use.

Hunting

Hunting in dinosaur times would have been a sight to behold. Meat-eaters used sharp claws and teeth to kill their victims. Sometimes packs of predators hunted together, combining their strength to bring down larger prey. Others hunted alone, relying on size and skill to take down their target.

Huge tail could be used as a powerful whip for defence.

At 13 m (43 ft) long, Giganotosaurus was larger than a T. rex.

Safety in numbers

Some plant-eating dinosaurs travelled in groups for protection. Together they could spot approaching predators more easily, like a herd of zebras might today. Predators find it harder to attack a large group because they need to single out a target.

Brachylophosaurus herd

Battle of the giants
Although Argentinosaurus was one of the biggest dinosaurs ever discovered, Giganotosaurus could cause serious damage, especially to young or injured individuals. It may have hunted in packs to bring down larger adults.

Argentinosaurus was slow, meaning running away was not an option.

Serrated teeth were perfect for slicing through skin.

Theropod dinosaurs, like Giganotosaurus, ran quickly on two powerful back legs.

Colour

Fossilized bones cannot give us information about the colour of dinosaurs. However, throughout the animal kingdom, brightly coloured feathers or skin are known to instantly attract attention. Dinosaurs like Citipati may have showed off in the same way.

Frills

Meat-eating Cryolophosaurus didn't need a frill for protection. Instead, it is likely that its crest was brightly coloured and used for display. It may have appealed to females and scared away rivals. Many ceratopsians had frills for the same reason.

The cassowary's large head crest and multicoloured skin ensure this flightless bird never goes unnoticed.

The Atlantic royal flycatcher has a showy forward-facing head frill.

Showing off

In prehistoric times there was fierce competition to attract a mate, just like there is now. Dinosaurs developed special features to show themselves off to potential partners. Many millions of years later, animals today use similar tactics to stand out from the crowd and catch the eye of the opposite sex.

Nose

Not much is known about dinosaur mating calls, but Muttaburrasaurus might have used them to impress females. It had a bony bump on its nose that may have had an inflatable crest attached to it! This would have made its calls reverberate, so they were louder.

The elephant seal uses its inflatable nose to amplify its mating roars, so they sound even louder.

Horns

Prominent horns might have been used as weapons when fighting rival dinosaurs for females and territory. Like many ceratopsians, Pentaceratops had long brow horns that males may have battled each other with.

Male deer, called stags, grow big antlers to do battle with rivals during the mating season.

Male and female

The limited information about dinosaur colour means we don't know if males and females looked the same. However, lots of male birds use a rainbow of colours to get a female's attention. Male mallards, a type of duck, have shiny green heads and purple streaked wings in contrast with the duller brown females.

Female and male mallards

Eggs

Like many of the dinosaurs themselves, eggs were often enormous. They were covered in hard shells like a chicken's egg, but were shaped differently. Although large, eggs were often much smaller than adult dinosaurs, so babies must have grown fast.

Citipati

18 cm (7 in) long

Citipati egg
Fossil finds show that beaked Citipati laid at least 20 oval eggs in a nest. These eggs were as big as a human hand. Recent research has shown that Citipati eggs were a blue-green colour.

Troodon

14 cm (5½ in) long

Troodon egg
Many fossilized Troodon eggs have been found. This meat-eating dinosaur may have laid as many as 24 eggs in a single nest, which were partly covered in plants to help keep them warm.

Hen

5 cm (2 in) long

Chicken egg
Female chickens, or hens, lay small, hard-shelled eggs. They keep the eggs warm for about 21 days until the chick hatches.

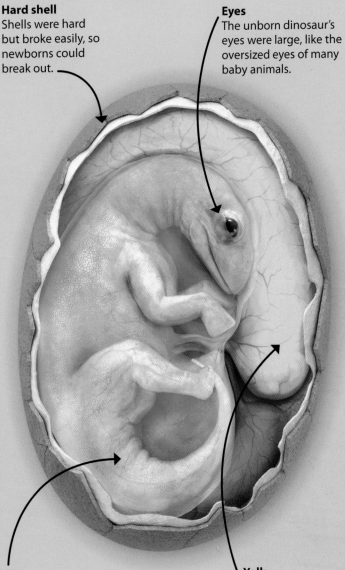

Hypacrosaurus

20 cm (8 in) long

Hypacrosaurus
The large eggs of plant-eating Hypacrosaurus were almost as big as a football. But even bigger dinosaur eggs have been found, which are more than twice the size of a Hypacrosaurus egg!

Nesting

Female dinosaurs often laid their eggs together in groups called clutches. Some made a nest covered in plant matter or earth for warmth, while others sat on the eggs and protected them. Some dinosaurs nested near each other for safety.

Hadrosaur nest

Inside an egg

In rare cases, the skeletons of unborn baby dinosaurs are found inside their fossilized eggs. This helps identify which dinosaur laid the eggs and gives an amazing chance to see what these babies would have looked like.

Hard shell
Shells were hard but broke easily, so newborns could break out.

Eyes
The unborn dinosaur's eyes were large, like the oversized eyes of many baby animals.

Sac
A thin, stretchy sheet called the "amniotic sac" protects the unborn baby.

Yolk
A bag of food called the yolk feeds the unborn dinosaur.

Parenting

Some dinosaurs were good parents, treating their eggs and babies with great care and attention. Fossils have shown that a few parents stayed with their eggs to keep them warm and to protect them against predators. When the eggs hatched, these dinosaurs fed and helped their young until they became able to look after themselves.

Staying safe

Today there are plenty of good parents in the animal kingdom. Crocodile mothers carry their babies from the nest to the safety of the water, while ostrich mothers and fathers watch over their chicks in a group, like children in a nursery.

A mother crocodile carefully holds a baby in her mouth.

Baby ostriches stay in a group for safety.

A baby Citipati would have used its beak to crack through its eggshell.

Citipati

In the 1990s this fossilized Citipati was found guarding its eggs, and was nicknamed "Big Mama". Its position is like a modern bird sitting on its eggs in a nest. Citipati was a feathered dinosaur and it may have been incubating its eggs, keeping them warm until they hatched. Later research has shown this dinosaur was probably the father, not the mother, of the eggs.

A protective, feathery arm is placed around the eggs to keep them warm.

The eggs have hard shells, similar to a modern bird's eggs.

The legs are bent back because the father is squatting down.

REALLY?

A desert sandstorm or heavy rainfall probably killed this father and his babies.

Baby dinosaurs

Remains of young dinosaurs reveal how babies grew and changed into adults. Like most young animals, baby dinosaurs had oversized heads, eyes, and feet until their bodies caught up in size. Although they started small, babies grew quickly and became fully grown dinosaurs in just a few years.

Flat skull and large eyes

Scaly, patterned skin

Baby Maiasaura

Newly hatched Maiasaura stayed in their nest to keep warm and grow strong. Their mother brought plants and leaves for them to eat. The babies were only 30 cm (12 in) long at birth, but a year later, they were 3 m (10 ft) long.

1. The skeletons of some tiny newborn dinosaurs could fit in a human's hand.

2. Baby duck-billed dinosaurs, like Maiasaura, doubled in size in just six weeks.

3. Apatosaurus babies had to gain 14 kg (30 lb) of weight a day to reach their adult size of 18 tonnes (19.8 tons).

At 9 m (30 ft) long, the mother Maiasaura was the same length as a bus.

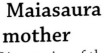

Maiasaura mother

Discoveries of the fossilized remains of adult Maiasaura next to hundreds of nests, eggs, and young show that the mothers looked after their babies. This is why this dinosaur was given the name Maiasaura, as it means "good mother lizard".

Growing up

The fossilized remains of large groups of Protoceratops have been found in deserts in Asia. The skulls show how their heads changed in shape and size as these dinosaurs grew up.

Hatchling skull
The skull of a baby Protoceratops shows the basic head shape, including the eye sockets and a tiny neck frill.

Juvenile skull
As Protoceratops starts to grow up, its beak gets longer, helping it to feed on plants.

Sub-adult skull
The cheeks have become wider and the beak more narrow. The neck frill is more developed.

Adult skull
The fully grown Protoceratops skull has a strong neck frill and large cheek horns. Adults were about the size of a sheep.

>> Scale

Adult Protoceratops

Feathers

Modern birds are the best known feathery animals. However, experts have found fossilized feathers, which proves that dinosaurs were feathered too. Dinosaurs developed feathers on their bodies for warmth, protection, and for display, a long time before they were used for flight.

A feathery crest may have attracted mates.

Velociraptor

In 2007, palaeontologists re-examined a Velociraptor fossil and discovered little bumps on its arm bones. The feathers of birds today sprout from similar bumps, called quill knobs, suggesting Velociraptor had long feathers on its arms.

Long feathers on arm.

Feather types

The first dinosaur feathers were simple structures like strands of hair. They provided warmth, attracted mates, and might have worked as camouflage, helping the dinosaur to hide. Over time, feathers developed into more complicated forms until they were ready for flight.

Hollow hair-like feather shape

Bristles
From scaly skin, dinosaurs like Heterodontosaurus grew basic hair-like feathers with a bristly texture. They were hollow, with nothing inside them.

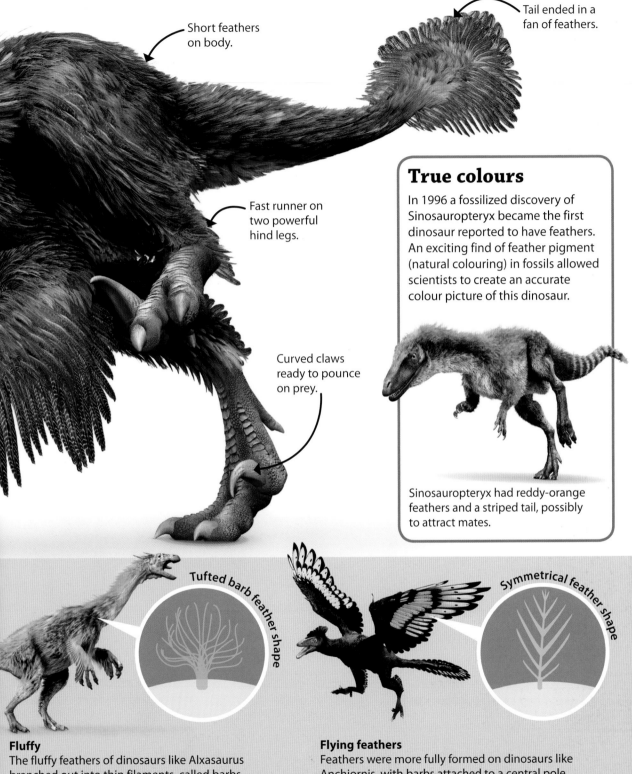

Short feathers on body.

Tail ended in a fan of feathers.

Fast runner on two powerful hind legs.

Curved claws ready to pounce on prey.

True colours

In 1996 a fossilized discovery of Sinosauropteryx became the first dinosaur reported to have feathers. An exciting find of feather pigment (natural colouring) in fossils allowed scientists to create an accurate colour picture of this dinosaur.

Sinosauropteryx had reddy-orange feathers and a striped tail, possibly to attract mates.

Tufted barb feather shape

Symmetrical feather shape

Fluffy
The fluffy feathers of dinosaurs like Alxasaurus branched out into thin filaments, called barbs, from a single point on the skin.

Flying feathers
Feathers were more fully formed on dinosaurs like Anchiornis, with barbs attached to a central pole. This dinosaur might have been able to glide.

Sea and sky

Dinosaurs stole the show in the prehistoric world, but they weren't the only reptiles around. Pterosaurs flew in the skies and sea-dwelling reptiles swam in the oceans. Marine reptiles included plesiosaurs, such as Albertonectes, and ichthyosaurs, such as Stenopterygius.

Its wingspan measured up to 1 m (3 ft).

Rhamphorhynchus

The flying Rhamphorhynchus took to the skies in the Jurassic period. This fish-eating reptile used its wings to soar over coasts and rivers hunting for prey.

Pointed teeth could hold tight to slippery squid.

Four flippers were used like paddles.

Albertonectes

This ocean swimmer had a neck longer than the rest of its body, with a record-breaking 76 neck bones. Flapping its flippers, Albertonectes could look along the seabed for shellfish or grab passing fish and squid.

Elasmosaurus

Long and lean, Elasmosaurus was a plesiosaur measuring around 9 m (30 ft). It swam slowly in the ocean, using its firm flippers to push itself through the water while hunting for fish.

Pterodaustro

This reptile lived and hunted by the beach. Pterodaustro was a filter feeder, scooping up water in its big beak and straining it to leave behind small sea creatures.

A long, curved beak held about 1,000 teeth.

The large wings were well-adapted for flight.

Quetzalcoatlus

One of the largest animals to ever take flight, Quetzalcoatlus had a wingspan of 10 m (33 ft), the same as a small plane. It was about the same size as an adult giraffe.

The raised head crest might have been colourful.

The large wings were made of stretched skin.

Stenopterygius

As sleek as a dolphin, Stenopterygius sped through the seas at speeds topping 50 kph (31 mph). There was no escape for the fish or squid that found themselves caught in its toothy snout.

A tail fin pushed Stenopterygius through the water.

Liopleurodon

The king of the seas in Jurassic times, Liopleurodon was a whopping 7 m (23 ft) long. This giant hunter killed marine life with its huge teeth and had no predators.

Its nose could smell prey underwater.

WOW!

Albertonectes grew up to **11 m (36 ft) long,** which is as long as a bus.

End of the dinosaurs

The age of the dinosaurs came to an explosive end 66 million years ago. Disaster struck when a huge rock from space smashed into planet Earth. At the same time massive volcanic eruptions released poisonous gases into the air. These events caused such an extreme change in the weather that many plants and animals died in one mass extinction.

Flying reptiles
Pterosaurs had ruled the skies for millions of years, but not one survived the extinction.

Dinosaurs
After 169 million years on Earth, the dinosaurs were wiped out in a very short space of time. They were badly affected by the cold temperatures.

Marine reptiles
None of the big reptiles that lived in the oceans survived the conditions after the meteorite hit.

Meteorite strikes!

Rocks from space that hit the Earth are called meteorites. Experts believe this meteorite measured a massive 10 km (6 miles) across. As well as killing nearby animals, the dust it caused stopped sunlight reaching the ground, causing the Earth to cool and plants to die.

Who died?

About 70 per cent of all life on Earth ended. No animal on land bigger than a dog survived the destruction. Fewer plants meant large herbivores starved and that meant less food for big carnivores.

Birds
Only 25 per cent of bird types survived the mass extinction. They are now the closest living relatives of dinosaurs.

Mammals
Most mammal groups managed to cling on during the extinction. They quickly took advantage of the disappearance of their dinosaur predators.

Invertebrates
Although many invertebrates were killed, the survivors bounced back. Today there are more invertebrates than any other type of animal.

Amphibians
Amphibians, like frogs, were lucky. It seems they were unaffected by the huge changes around them. Perhaps because they were small and could hide away.

Reptiles
Snakes, lizards, and turtles survived. Freshwater crocodiles were some of the largest survivors of the extinction in terms of size.

Who survived?
Some animal groups managed to adapt to the new conditions and we can still see their relatives today. With no dinosaurs to eat them, mammals grew to sizes they were never able to before.

Fish
Deep below the surface, smaller fish avoided the effects of the changes in weather.

Deinonychus

With its large, sharp claws and teeth, Deinonychus was a Cretaceous killer. This theropod dinosaur could run at high speeds and do a lot of damage with its weaponry. It is one of the dinosaurs most closely related to modern birds.

» **Length:** 3 m (10 ft)

» **Weight:** 80 kg (175 lb)

» **Diet:** Meat

» **Habitat:** Woodland

The small head crest may have been for display.

Two clawed feet were used for walking.

Sharp talons could rip flesh.

Feathers covered Deinonychus.

Distant relatives

Chickens have dense feathers, which keep them warm and protect their skin.

You may not expect to see birds on a dinosaur's family tree, but they are their closest living relatives. In fact, birds are dinosaurs! During the Jurassic period, some meat-eating theropod dinosaurs developed into feathered fliers and although many of these birds died out in the mass extinction, some survived and have been flying high ever since.

A toothless, horny beak replaced the terrifying teeth.

Large crest attracts mates.

Stepping stones

Dinosaurs and birds may look completely different, but small changes over millions of years have had some big effects. Feathered dinosaurs took many different forms before becoming the birds we recognize today.

Short, feathered wings

Archaeopteryx
Alive in the Jurassic, one of the earliest bird-like dinosaurs was Archaeopteryx. It had the head, clawed hands, and tail of a dinosaur, but the wings of a bird. These wings were too weak for anything more than brief flight.

Long tail feathers

Confuciusornis
By Cretaceous times, dinosaurs like Confuciusornis were even more like modern birds. The teeth and tail had gone, replaced by a toothless beak and flapping wings, though flying still proved challenging.

Short tail

Iberomesornis
The later Cretaceous period saw sparrow-sized Iberomesornis arrive. With large chest muscles and a short tail, taking flight was smoother and easier.

FACT FILE

Chicken

Like all birds, chickens are the descendants of dinosaurs. These small birds share many of the features passed on from their giant ancestors, including feathered bodies, clawed feet, light bones, and hard-shelled eggs.

» **Length:** 0.4 m (16 in)

» **Weight:** 3 kg (7 lb)

» **Diet:** Plants, insects, and seeds

» **Habitat:** Farmland and forests

Chickens rarely use their wings for flight.

The clawed feet have no feathers.

New dinosaurs

Although they died at least 66 million years ago, new dinosaurs are still being discovered all the time. Once a fossil has been dug up, scientists need to check it and see if it should be named as a new type of dinosaur, which might take years. Who knows what odd fossil finds are yet to be made!

The fossilized skull of Aquilops fits in a human hand.

Aquilops

A skull the size of a rabbit's turned out to be the earliest ceratopsian from North America. Aquilops was a four-legged plant-eater from the Cretaceous period with a strange spike on its nose.

NAMED
2014

A bird-like beak gives Aquilops its name, which means "eagle face".

NAMED
2014

Anzu stood 3 m (10 ft) tall.

The long feathery tail measured 1 m (3 ft).

Anzu

An unusual dinosaur recently revealed in a rocky area called the Hell Creek Formation in North America has been nicknamed "the chicken from Hell". This bird-like dinosaur had a toothless beak, feathery body, and sharp claws.

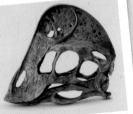
Skull of Anzu showing head crest.

The hump
may have been
a fat store or
used for display.

Concavenator

An almost complete
skeleton found in Spain,
measuring 6 m (20 ft),
belonged to a theropod
from the Cretaceous
period. Concavenator
stands out from other
two-legged meat-eaters because
of its distinctive humped back.

NAMED
2010

Concavenator skeleton

Most colours given to
drawings of dinosaurs
are guesswork by
the artist.

Regaliceratops skull fossil

Regaliceratops

A new ceratopsian discovered
in Canada is a close relative
of Triceratops. A dramatic
crown-like frill gives
Regaliceratops its name, which
means "royal horned face".

NAMED
2015

Dinosaur facts and figures

Dinosaurs were a fascinating group of reptiles. Here are some weird and wonderful facts you might not know about them!

TROODON is thought to have been the most clever dinosaur because it had a large brain compared to its relatively small size.

The **most expensive dinosaur fossil** in the world is the **skeleton of "Sue" the T. rex**, which cost the The Field Museum of Natural History in Chicago, USA, **$8,362,000**!

Compsognathus had a top speed of 64 kph (40 mph), which is faster than an Olympic sprinter.

12

is how old the English fossil hunter Mary Anning was when she found the first ichthyosaur, a type of ancient marine reptile.

2,300

The first dinosaur discovery might have been as long as 2,300 years ago, when a Chinese man called Chang Qu wrote about finding some "dragon" bones.

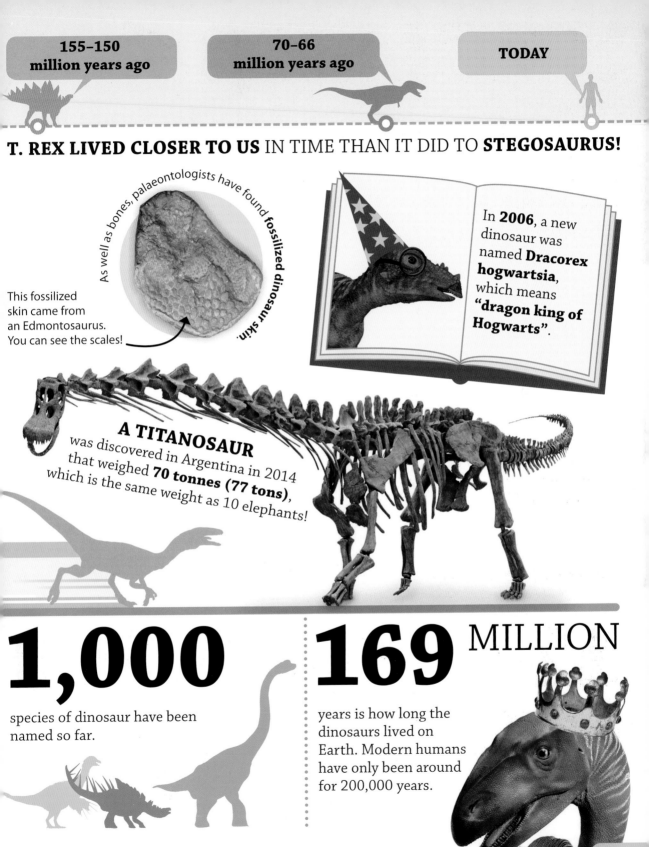

T. REX LIVED CLOSER TO US IN TIME THAN IT DID TO STEGOSAURUS!

As well as bones, palaeontologists have found **fossilized dinosaur skin**.

This fossilized skin came from an Edmontosaurus. You can see the scales!

In **2006**, a new dinosaur was named **Dracorex hogwartsia**, which means **"dragon king of Hogwarts"**.

A TITANOSAUR was discovered in Argentina in 2014 that weighed **70 tonnes (77 tons)**, which is the same weight as 10 elephants!

1,000

species of dinosaur have been named so far.

169 MILLION

years is how long the dinosaurs lived on Earth. Modern humans have only been around for 200,000 years.

Before dinosaurs

By 310 MYA there were reptiles, amphibians, invertebrates, and fish. Trilobites, woodlouse-like sea creatures, died out before the dinosaurs even appeared.

» 235 million years ago

First dinosaurs

The earliest dinosaurs appeared around 235 MYA. Dinosaurs like Eoraptor lived alongside other huge reptiles.

» 130 MYA

Iguanodon

This dinosaur existed for about five million years in the Cretaceous period.

» 140 MYA

First ceratopsians

These horned dinosaurs made their entrance in the Early Cretaceous.

» 155 MYA

First birds

Archaeopteryx was one of the first birds.

» 125 MYA

First flowering plants

The first flowers were small compared to ones today. By 100 MYA many recognizable flowers were blooming, such as magnolias.

» 112 MYA

Spinosaurus

Spinosaurus walked the Earth for five million years in the Cretaceous.

» 100 MYA

First bees

Once flowers had appeared so did flower-loving insects such as bees.

Dinosaurs and us

» 30 MYA

First cats

Early cats were meat-eaters, just like cats today.

Dinosaurs existed for almost 170 million years, but this is just a moment in the 3.8 billion years of life on Earth. A huge range of animals and plants appeared before, alongside, and after them. Once dinosaurs had disappeared, other types of animal, like mammals, took over.

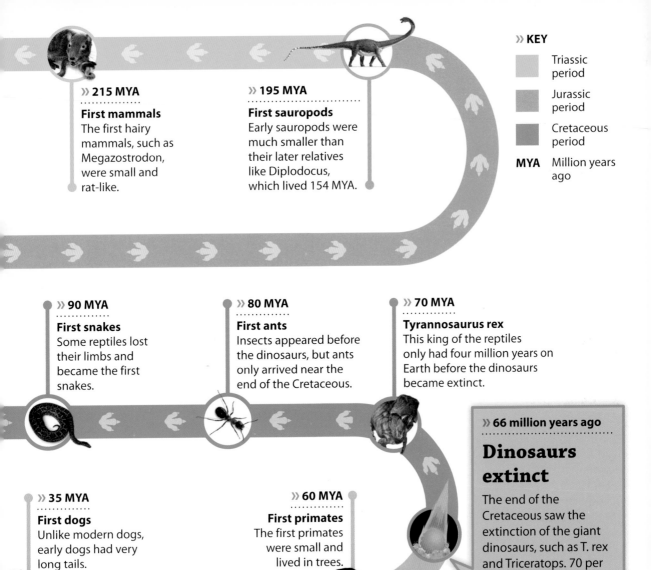

215 MYA

First mammals
The first hairy mammals, such as Megazostrodon, were small and rat-like.

195 MYA

First sauropods
Early sauropods were much smaller than their later relatives like Diplodocus, which lived 154 MYA.

90 MYA

First snakes
Some reptiles lost their limbs and became the first snakes.

80 MYA

First ants
Insects appeared before the dinosaurs, but ants only arrived near the end of the Cretaceous.

70 MYA

Tyrannosaurus rex
This king of the reptiles only had four million years on Earth before the dinosaurs became extinct.

» 66 million years ago

Dinosaurs extinct

The end of the Cretaceous saw the extinction of the giant dinosaurs, such as T. rex and Triceratops. 70 per cent of all animals and plants were wiped out.

35 MYA

First dogs
Unlike modern dogs, early dogs had very long tails.

60 MYA

First primates
The first primates were small and lived in trees.

» 7 million years ago

First humans

Seven million years ago there was more than one type of human-like animal. Modern humans didn't appear until as recently as 200,000 years ago.

Modern humans

There are now more than seven billion people living on Earth. Humans live on all seven continents and have even made the leap into space! Now to see into the ancient past we have to look for fossils and other remains of prehistoric animals.

How to say it

This guide will show you how to say each dinosaur's name and what it means. Capital letters mean you should say that part of the name a tiny bit louder.

Albertosaurus
(Al-BERT-oh-SAW-rus)
lizard from Alberta

Allosaurus
(Al-uh-SAW-rus)
different lizard

Alxasaurus
(Al-xa-SAW-rus)
Alxa Desert lizard

Anchiornis
(ANG-kee-OR-niss)
nearby bird

Ankylosaurus
(an-KYE-low-SAW-rus)
fused lizard

Anzu
(an-ZOO)
feathered demon

Apatosaurus
(a-PAT-oh-SAW-rus)
deceptive lizard

Aquilops
(ah-QUILL-ops)
eagle face

Archaeopteryx
(ar-kee-OP-ter-ix)
ancient wing

Argentinosaurus
(AHR-jen-TEEN-uh-SAW-rus)
Argentina lizard

Barosaurus
(BARE-uh-SAW-rus)
heavy lizard

Brachiosaurus
(BRACK-ee-oh-SAW-rus)
armed lizard

Chindesaurus
(CHIN-dee-SAW-rus)
lizard from Chinde Point

Citipati
(sit-ih-PA-tee)
lord of the funeral pyre

Coelophysis
(see-lo-FISE-iss)
hollow form

Compsognathus
(KOMP-SOW-NAY-thus)
pretty jaw

Concavenator
(KON-cav-ee-nah-tor)
predator from Cuenca

Confuciusornis
(KON-FYOO-shi-SOR-nis)
Confucius bird

Cryolophosaurus
(KRIE-ol-lof-oh-SAW-rus)
frozen-crested lizard

Deinonychus
(dye-NON-ik-us)
terrible claw

Diplodocus
(dip-LOD-oh-kus)
double-beamed

Dracorex hogwartsia
(DRAK-o-rex HOG-wart-cia)
dragon king of Hogwarts

Dreadnoughtus
(dread-NOUGHT-iss)
fears nothing

Edmontosaurus
(ed-MONT-oh-SAW-rus)
Edmonton lizard

Einiosaurus
(eye-nee-oh-SAW-rus)
buffalo lizard

Eocursor
(ee-oh-KUHR-sor)
dawn runner

Eoraptor
(ee-oh-RAP-tor)
dawn raptor

Euoplocephalus
(you-op-luh-SEF-uh-lus)
well-armoured lizard

Giganotosaurus
(gi-GAN-oh-toh-SAW-rus)
giant southern lizard

Giraffatitan
(gi-RAF-a-TIE-tan)
giant giraffe

Gojirasaurus
(go-JEER-a-SAW-rus)
Godzilla lizard

Herrerasaurus
(huh-REHR-uh-SAW-rus)
Herrera's lizard

Heterodontosaurus
(hett-er-o-don-toe-SAW-rus)
different-toothed lizard

Huayangosaurus
(hwah-YAHNG-o-SAW-rus)
Huayang lizard

Hypacrosaurus
(hi-PAK-ro-SAW-rus)
near the highest lizard

Hypsilophodon
(hip-see-LOAF-oh-don)
high-crested tooth

Iberomesornis
(eye-BER-oh-mes-OR-nis)
Spanish intermediate bird

Iguanodon
(ig-WA-no-DON)
iguana tooth

Kentrosaurus
(KEN-truh-SAW-rus)
spiked lizard

Maiasaura
(mah-ee-ah-SAW-ruh)
good mother lizard

Megalosaurus
(MEG-a-low-SAW-rus)
great lizard

Mussaurus
(mus-SAW-rus)
mouse lizard

Muttaburrasaurus
(mut-tah-BUR-rah-SAW-rus)
Muttaburra lizard

Ouranosaurus
(oo-RAN-oh-SAW-rus)
brave lizard

Pachycephalosaurus
(PAK-ee-KEF-al-oh-SAW-rus)
thick-headed lizard

Pentaceratops
(PEN-ta-SER-a-tops)
five-horned face

Parasaurolophus
(par-a-SAW-roh-LOAF-us)
near crested lizard

Pisanosaurus
(pye-SAN-uh-SAW-rus)
Pisano lizard

Plateosaurus
(PLAY-tee-uh-SAW-rus)
broad lizard

Protoceratops
(PRO-toe-SER-a-tops)
first horned face

Regaliceratops
(ree-GUH-li-SER-a-tops)
royal horned face

Saltasaurus
(SALT-a-SAW-rus)
Salta area lizard

Scutellosaurus
(scoo-TEL-oh-SAW-rus)
little shield lizard

Sinosauropteryx
(SINE-oh-soh-ROP-tuh-riks)
Chinese reptilian wing

Staurikosaurus
(STORE-ee-koh-SAW-rus)
Southern Cross lizard

Spinosaurus
(SPINE-oh-SAW-rus)
spiny lizard

Stegosaurus
(STEG-o-SAW-rus)
roof lizard

Suchomimus
(SOOK-o-MY-mus)
crocodile mimic

Thecodontosaurus
(thee-co-DON-toe-SAW-rus)
socket tooth lizard

Therizinosaurus
(thair-uh-ZEEN-uh-SAW-rus)
scythe lizard

Triceratops
(try-SER-a-tops)
three-horned face

Troodon
(TROH-o-don)
wounding tooth

Tyrannosaurus rex
(tie-RAN-oh-SAW-rus rex)
tyrant lizard king

Udanoceratops
(oo-DAHN-o-SER-a-tops)
Udan-Sayr horn face

Velociraptor
(vel-o-si-RAP-tor)
speedy thief

Glossary

Here are the meanings of some words that are useful to know when learning about dinosaurs.

Dinosaurs lay eggs.

ankylosaurs Plant-eating dinosaurs with four legs and body armour, such as plates and spikes. They lived in the Cretaceous period

armour Naturally hard body covering that provides protection for an animal

camouflage Colours or patterns on an animal's skin, fur, or feathers that help it merge with the environment

carnivore Animal that eats only meat

ceratopsians Plant-eating dinosaurs with four legs, horns, and beaks. They lived in the Jurassic and Cretaceous periods

conifer Type of tree with needle-like leaves

coprolite Animal droppings that have become fossilized

Cretaceous period Third and final period of the Mesozoic Era, from 145 to 66 million years ago

erosion Gradual wearing away of rocks due to weather

fossil Remains of a dead dinosaur or other animal, which has been preserved in rock over time

fossilization Process by which an animal or plant becomes a fossil

hadrosaurs Plant-eating dinosaurs with duck bills, and sometimes, bony crests. They lived in the Cretaceous period

herbivore Animal that eats only plant matter

ichthyosaur Type of marine reptile with the shape of a dolphin, alive in the Mesozoic Era

incubate Keeping eggs warm until they hatch

invertebrate Animal without a backbone

Jurassic period Second period of the Mesozoic Era, from 201 to 145 million years ago

mammals Warm-blooded vertebrate animals that have skin covered in hair and feed their offspring milk

Einiosaurus is a ceratopsian.

mass extinction Death of a large number of dinosaur, animal, or plant species at the same time

Mesozoic Era Triassic, Jurassic, and Cretaceous periods together

meteorite Rock from space that crashes into Earth

omnivore Animal that eats both plant matter and meat

ornithopods Plant-eating dinosaurs that stood on two legs. They lived in the Jurassic and Cretaceous periods

pachycephalosaurs Plant-eating or omnivorous dinosaurs with two legs and domed skulls. They lived in the Cretaceous period

palaeontologist Scientist who studies fossilized finds, including dinosaurs, animals, and plants

Pangaea Huge supercontinent that existed on Earth at the start of the Mesozoic Era

plesiosaur Type of marine reptile that usually had a long neck, alive in the Mesozoic Era

predator Dinosaur or other animal that hunts other living animals for food

prehistoric Ancient time before recorded history

preserved Remains that have not changed much over time

prey Dinosaur or other animal that is hunted for food

primate Group of mammals that includes monkeys, apes, and humans

pterosaurs Large, flying reptiles of the Mesozoic Era

reptiles Cold-blooded animals with scaly skin that reproduce by laying eggs. This group includes snakes, lizards, crocodiles, and dinosaurs

sauropods Huge plant-eating dinosaurs on four legs with long necks and small heads. They lived in the Triassic, Jurassic, and Cretaceous periods

scavenger Dinosaur or other animal that feeds on the leftover meat of another animal that has already died, whether by a predator attack or natural causes

serrated Having a sharp, jagged edge

solitary An animal that lives alone

species Specific types of dinosaurs, animals, or plants with shared features that can mate and produce young together

stegosaurs Plant-eating dinosaurs with four legs and plates or spines down their backs. They lived in the Jurassic and Cretaceous periods

theropods Meat-eating dinosaurs that hunted on two legs. They lived in the Triassic, Jurassic, and Cretaceous periods, and were the ancestors of birds

Triassic period First of three periods in the Mesozoic Era, from 252 to 201 million years ago

vegetation Plant life found in a particular habitat

vertebrate Animal with a backbone

Index

Acknowledgements

The publisher would like to thank the following people for their assistance: Ruth O'Rourke and Kathleen Teece for editorial assistance, Alexandra Beeden for proofreading, Helen Peters for compiling the index, Neeraj Bhatia for cutouts, Peter Minister and Andrew Kerr for CGI artwork, and Dan Crisp and Ed Merritt for illustrations. The publishers would also like to thank Dr Kenneth Lacovara for the "Meet the expert" interview.

The publisher would like to thank the following for their kind permission to reproduce their photographs:

(Key: a-above; b-below/bottom; c-centre; f-far; l-left; r-right; t-top)

6 **Getty Images:** Bradley Kanaris / Stringer (crb). 7 **Corbis:** Tom Bean (bl). 8-9 **Dorling Kindersley:** Dan Crisp. 11 **Getty Images:** Nigel Dennis (br). 14 **Dorling Kindersley:** Oxford Museum of Natural History (tc). 15 **Corbis:** Darrell Gulin (cra). 20 **Dorling Kindersley:** Natural History Museum, London (cra). 20-21 **Alamy Images:** Nobumichi Tamura / Stocktrek Images (b). 21 **Alamy Images:** The Natural History Museum (cra). 22 **Alamy Images:** Kostyantyn Ivanyshen / Stocktrek Images (clb). 24 **Corbis:** Louie Psihoyos (cr). **Dorling Kindersley:** The American Museum of Natural History (cla). 25 **Alamy Images:** Bosiljka Zutich (cb). **Corbis:** Corbis Wire (cra). 26-27 **Dorling Kindersley**: Dan Crisp. 27 **Corbis**: Scientifica (cra). 28 **Dr. Kenneth Lacovara:** (tr, bl). 29 **Dr. Kenneth Lacovara:** (tr). 30-31 **Alamy Images:** Jim Lane. 30 **Corbis:** Walter Geiersperger (br). 31 **Corbis:** Walter Geiersperger (bc). 32 **Getty Images:** Photographer's Choice RF / Jon Boyes (plates). 34-35 **Corbis:** Nik Wheeler (background). 36 **Alamy Images:** Octavio Campos Salles (crb). **Corbis:** Daryl Benson / Masterfile (cb). 37 **Corbis:** Nigel Pavitt / JAI (clb). **Dorling Kindersley:** British Wildlife Centre, Surrey, UK (crb). **naturepl.com:** Visuals Unlimited (bc). 39 **Science Photo Library:** Sinclair Stammers (clb). 40-41 **Corbis:** Louie Psihoyos. 40 **Alamy Images:** Nature Picture Library (tc/crocodile). **Corbis:** Richard Du Toit / Minden Pictures (tc). 43 **Dorling Kindersley:** The American Museum of Natural History / Lynton Gardiner (c/all skulls). 52 **Andrew A. Farke / Sam Noble Oklahoma Museum of Natural History:** (cra). **Getty Images:** Handout (bl). 53 **Alamy Images**: Rick Rudnicki (crb). **Getty Images:** AFP / Stringer (cra). 54 **Alamy Images:** Pictorial Press Ltd (bc). **Dorling Kindersley:** Dan Crisp (cl) 55 **Alamy Images:** chrisstockphotography (c); Corey Ford (cra). 57 **123RF.com:** Anna Omelchenko (br)

Cover images: *Front:* **Corbis:** Walter Geiersperger fcr; **Dorling Kindersley:** Oxford Museum of Natural History fcra; *Back:* **Corbis:** Walter Geiersperger tl; **Dorling Kindersley:** The American Museum of Natural History cla; **Front Flap: Alamy Images:** chrisstockphotography, Rick Rudnicki clb; **Dorling Kindersley:** Natural History Museum, London bc; **Getty Images**: Handout cra; **Back Flap: Dorling Kindersley:** Natural History Museum, London crb, The University of Aberdeen cl; **NASA:** clb; **Front Endpapers: Dorling Kindersley:** The Natural History Museum, London tc; **Back Endpapers: Ed Merritt** (All earth images)

All other images © Dorling Kindersley
For further information see:
www.dkimages.com

My Findout facts:

How the world changed

Triassic

252–201 MILLION YEARS AGO

The centre of Pangaea is a sizzling desert with few animals.

PANGAEA

The sea surrounding the continent is called Panthalassa.

The Triassic period began after a mass extinction killed 90 per cent of the life previously on Earth. Pangaea was Earth's only continent, but it covered an enormous area. New forms of life arrived, including the first dinosaurs and small mammals.

DINOSAURS

Chindesaurus	Mussaurus
Coelophysis	Pisanosaurus
Eocursor	Plateosaurus
Eoraptor	Staurikosaurus
Gojirasaurus	Thecodontosaurus
Herrerasaurus	

Jurassic

201–145 MILLION YEARS AGO

LAURASIA

GONDWANA

Pangaea is breaking up to create North America, Europe, and Asia.

Warm weather melts the ice at the North and South poles.

Following another mass extinction at the end of the Triassic, dinosaurs took over the Jurassic period. They grew bigger and stronger, with giant sauropods feasting on trees and hungry meat-eaters on the prowl. Pangaea split into two smaller continents, Laurasia and Gondwana.

DINOSAURS

Allosaurus	Diplodocus
Apatosaurus	Heterodontosaurus
Archaeopteryx	Kentrosaurus
Barosaurus	Megalosaurus
Brachiosaurus	Stegosaurus
Cryolophosaurus	